The Lower Provinces

DANIEL O'LEARY

The Lower Provinces

Cover art by J. W. Stewart.
Author photograph by Sara O'Leary.
Book designed and typeset by Primeau Barey, Montreal.
Edited by Steve Luxton.

Copyright © Daniel O'Leary, 2012.
Legal Deposit, Bibliothèque et Archives nationales du Québec
and the National Library of Canada, 2nd trimester, 2012.

Library and Archives Canada Cataloguing in Publication
O'Leary, Daniel, 1961-
The lower provinces / Daniel O'Leary.
Poems.
ISBN 978-1-897190-82-1 (bound).
ISBN 978-1-897190-81-4 (pbk.)
1. Title.
PS8579.L28L69 2012   C811'.54   C2012-902331-0

This is a work of art. Names, characters, places, and events are either products
of the author's imagination or are employed fictitiously. Any resemblance to actual
events or locales or persons, living or dead, is entirely coincidental.

No part of this publication may be reproduced or stored in a retrieval system
or transmitted in any form or by any means, electronic, mechanical, recording,
or otherwise, without written permission of the publisher, DC Books.

In the case of photocopying or other reprographic copying, a license must be
obtained from Access Copyright, Canadian Copyright Licensing Agency,
1 Yonge Street, Suite 800, Toronto, Ontario M5E 1E5 <info@accesscopyright.ca>.

For our publishing activities, DC Books gratefully acknowledges the financial
support of the Canada Council for the Arts, of SODEC, and of the Government
of Canada through the Book Publishing Industry Development Program (BPIDP).

Canada Council   Conseil des Arts
for the Arts   du Canada

Société
de développement
des entreprises
culturelles

Québec

Printed and bound in Canada by Groupe Transcontinental.
Interior pages printed on FSC® certified environmentally responsible paper.
Distributed by LitDistCo.

MIX
Paper from
responsible sources
FSC   FSC® C011825

DC Books
PO Box 666, Station Saint-Laurent
Montreal, Quebec H4L 4V9
www.dcbooks.ca

Contents

1 Acknowledgements
3 Preface

British North America Suite
7 Of the Decadent Poets
8 The Mirror of Days (1897–1924)
9 After Anne Hébert
10 Documents from the Office of Professor Darey
17 Bishop Bompas in Chthonia
19 Mrs. Mary Coy Bradley
21 The Hanging of Samuel Lount and Peter Matthews
23 Lawren Harris's "Garden"
24 Remembering Aeneas McCharles
26 The Visitation of Margaret Blennerhasset, *Née* Agnew
27 The Haunting of Daniel O'Leary
28 Of Magi and Sage
James Evans, his Quotidiana, Moose Factory, 1832
29 The Emigration of Whitechapel Bess

Whig Histories
35 Millennial Poem for Canada
36 Strange Songs
38 Anti-poem One: Introductory
40 Anti-poem Two: The Visions of Harold Adams Innis
41 Anti-poem Three: On the Logic of Deep Time
42 Anti-poem Four: Eyelash under the Eyelid
44 Catholicon: a Universal Remedy
46 A Man Talks to Himself Versified
47 Cobalt: An Alternative to Space Programs

- 49 The Concubinage and Fornication
  of Phantom and Grub
- 50 Crowning of the Virgin
- 51 In the Early Times of Which We Speak
- 53 Guessing the Devil's Age
- 54 Dressed in Blue and Green
- 56 On a Theme by P. H. Gosse
- 57 Not All Poets Are Fools
- 58 Of Whig Histories
- 60 Karkara
- 62 X=Y
- 63 Frederick Edward Smyth's 1911 Centenary Lecture
- 67 A Laugh at Ludwig Wittgenstein:
  Dead Relations at Oxford
- 68 Notes to the Poems

Acknowledgements

I am indebted to numerous people for their comments on early drafts of these poems, and to others for inspiration and learned conversation. Particularly, I would mention mentors Jonathan Wisenthal, G. David Sheps, and John Wilson Foster whose friendship and guidance has been invaluable in my life and work. Andre Furlani, Erin Mouré, Walid Bitar, Derrick Sleep, Danny Guilbert and Frank Hayes, also deserve mention for their insightful conversation, and as readers or auditors of these poems in their early versions, sometimes with the superadded hazard of concertina music. I thank them all for their comments and fellowship. I am also in the debt of Canadian authors Rawi Hage and Madeleine Thien for their hospitality in providing a roof (and a stimulating library) to keep me dry while editing the poems during my semester professing literature at Concordia University in Montreal.

Especially, I thank editor Steve Luxton for his incisive and acute notes on drafts of the book. His comments were inevitably wise and contributed substantially to whatever virtue the book has.

I also acknowledge and appreciate the generous support of the Canada Council whose aid allowed the completion of this project.

Finally, and mostly, I thank Sara, Liam, and Euan, whose love and patience are the most important factors in any work of mine.

Preface

Although I have followed the practice of Stevens, and in composition avoided reading highly-mannered, or *strong* poets, *like* Wallace Stevens, I cannot avoid confessing that while editing this book, at least, I have worked amidst the white noise of technological consumerism in a temple built from echoes of several important and historic living poets. Geoffrey Hill, Seamus Heaney, Robert Bringhurst, Erin Mouré, Ciaran Carson, Margaret Atwood, and Brian Bartlett, all stand in danger of my petty larcenies, if only in matters of pitch or key. David Adams Richards' fiction is always reassuring. Any saliences in my own poems result from my efforts to emulate, however feebly, their examples. Of the dead, the list is too long to be just to them all. If not for the fear of being mistaken, I would mention Allen Ginsberg. And although I would set aside suggestions of poetic influence of the great man here (and use *this* sentence to set aside all Whitmanian misreadings of the great soul William Blake), Ginsberg also remains a great soul, and my acquaintance and conversations with him made me witness to transcendental literary process. So, God bless Allen as well. And all else who join the militant glee, jubilant in attrition, balladeers of as yet un-regenerate nations, and of songs of redemption and regeneration at the end of time.

British North America Suite

Of the Decadent Poets

After the French of Wilfrid Lalonde (1906).

They speak Greek, Arabic, Slavic,
And are seized by the least writing
If carried out in a strong bit of Sanscrit....
–L. V.

Sphinx squatting at the feet of sombre pyramids,
as you sleep through the buffetings of passing enigmas,
are your silent hopes profound? You are not stupid,
but stupefied: your glory is to stupefy.

With an ever-filling glass—as the Danaë
filled the casks—you are impotent still,
casks ever bottomless, your cups ever void,
void of poetry, and void of good sense.

Lovers of the heavy mists drizzling from clouds,
your eyes dazzling while the verities of clouds
are streaming with waves of light over you.
But I don't insist, nature shares your laws:
and if the clarity of day is made for eagles,
the densities of night best convene the owls.

The Mirror of Days (1897–1924)

Albert Lozeau, Montréalais, encouched in an hauteur,
alone reaching head to foot: nineteen, enchambered
by slow death, holding hard against escape,
instructing humility implacably, for the paralytic
in his dust of days and cinder of hours.

From my balcony, as *les calèches* pass,
I relive my rare *promenades,*
the minutes of respite allowed me,
on your sufferance provided seasonally.

In the moment of deliverance
I possess myself in a plenitude of being,
profoundly collected and asleep to desire,
mild–so as to take part in heaven beyond my window.

Escape from despair, from the sight of death, is the poem
alone allowed: to endure the thoughts of the prophet
of the vanity of all. In my words I am not alone,
and I suffer, a solitary soul in company with you,
my Imagined, who are with me now and ever.

Vanity!–all are extinguished, all expire, and all pass:
the star in its clarity, the world in proud orgasm,
and the man who fulfills the tumult of space,
measuring his grandeur with the planks of a coffin.

22 January 1901
Montreal, Canada.

After Anne Hébert

In a tranquil country
we have received the passion
of the world, our nude sword
in our two hands posed.

Our hearts ignore the day
while the fire in the stem always returns,
and its luminescence crosses
the shadow of our traits.

Supported before all feebleness,
the charity secures
only advancing apprehension
and confusion.

She invents a universe
of the first justice, and we have part
of that vocation
in the extreme vitality of our love.

The life and the death
in our recognition of rights of asylum
watches with the eyes of the blind,
and touches with precise hands.

Documents from the Office of Professor Darey

McGill College, 1871.

Professor P. J. Darey, M. A.
Commission Géologique du Canada,
Sagluk, P. Q.

To the Right Honourable the Lord Baron Bunsen,
President, Societé Impériale Géologique de Vienne, etc.

My Lord,

I believe you will be ready to acknowledge that ever since you first knew me no person was ever more backward in asking favours than myself. But an unexpected affliction obliges me to solicit your assistance to the extent of £80 for about six months' time, at the expiry of which I pledge myself faithfully to discharge the obligation. At that time the sum owing shall be added to the amount of my dues outstanding and a draught posted as quickly as the vagaries of Arctic mail permit. If, however, I am asking you to inconvenience yourself, let no necessities of mine influence you, for it would pain me greatly were I to think you were a sufferer through obliging me. Before I could prevail upon myself to write this I have endeavoured to obtain the money from people whom I myself on several occasions have obliged, but I regret to say without success. My own substance has been exhausted on outfitting this summer's crew, and commission funds are not readily available for *ex officio* junkets even when for geological purposes. Principal Dawson, whose work on geological evidence of scriptural truths is admired by Agassiz, has secured my lectureship in the French Language for another year when I return to Montreal, and a contract for another phrase book and student's companion, which he assures me will be *un livre en usage* at L'École Normale, but the publisher refuses any advance, and the work is tedious and enervating. Your Lordship will also remember my fondness for brandy and reflect upon the sad fact that Labrador tea sweetened with no molasses is the strongest liquor permitted us here until the sea lanes open. The lack of books here is also a great hardship for a bookish man.

Regretting that this step should be at all necessary,
I have the honour to be, my Lord, your Lordship's most obedient and humble servant,

P. J. Darey, M. A.,
Commission Géologique du Canada.

EXPRESSIONS IDIOMATIQUES ET PROVERBES
(MS leaves from P. J. Darey's *The Dominion Phrase Book*)

Le pays n'est pas peuplé à proportion de son étendue;
il s'en faut de beaucoup.
The country is not peopled in proportion to its extent;
it lacks most of it.

Il en veut à tout le monde.
He has a grudge against every body.

Je m'en prendrai à vous de tout ce qui pourra arriver.
I shall lay the blame on you for all that can happen.

Vous vous y prenez bien.
You manage well.

Je m'y prends ainsi.
I set about it in this way.

Trouver à redire.
To find fault with, to blame.

C'est à qui l'aura.
The strife is who shall have it.

Songez qu'il y va de votre fortune.
Consider that your fortune is at stake.

Tarder.
To long.

Il lui tarde de finir son ouvrage.
He longs to finish his work.

Il me tardait de vous voir.
I longed to see you.

Coucher en joue, mettre en joue.
To aim at (with a gun).

Je couche l'oiseau en joue,
I aim at the bird.

Il a tiré un coup de fusil.
He fired a gun.

Avoir beau.
To be in vain.

Nous avons beau soliciter, il ne nous accordera pas cette grâce.
It is in vain for us to solicit, he will not grant us that favour.

Il laisse beaucoup à désirer.
He fails much of satisfying.

Elle ne laisse rien à désirer.
She is defective in nothing.

Ce prince sait faire cas des hommes de mérite.
That prince knows how to value men of merit.

Sa bibliothèque est sens dessus dessous.
His library is topsy-turvey.

Savez-vous vous passer de livres?
Can you do without books?

En faisant cela, il m'a ri au nez.
In doing that he laughed in my face.

Sa fierté l'emporta sur ses intérêts.
His pride prevailed over his interests.

Cet homme est gris.
That man is half intoxicated.

La vertu n'y entre pour rien.
Virtue is entirely out of the question.

Je la lui garde bonne.
I have a rod in pickle for him.

Jouer de malheur.
To be unlucky at play.

Le soleil perce les nuages.
The sun breaks through the clouds.

Le soleil me donne dans les yeux.
The sun strikes in my eyes.

Cela porte coup.
That hits home.

C'en est fait de lui.
It is all over with him.

Je sais où tend votre discours.
I know the drift of your discourse.

La faim chasse le loup du bois.
Hunger will break through stone walls.

Argent fait tout.
Money makes the mare go.

Les gros poissons mangent les petits.
Might overcomes right.

Il s'en est allé à la dérobée.
He went away by stealth.

Elle a de beaux yeux, mais ils ne disent rien.
She has fine eyes but they want expression.

Entrons dans ce bois, nous serons à l'ombre.
Let us go in that wood, we shall be in the shade.

> Cadman Adamson,
> **Haberdasher, Hatter, and Purveyor,**
> Rye Lane, London.

July 20, 1871

Professor P. J. Darey, Esq.
McGill College Avenue,
Montreal, Province of Quebec,
Dominion of Canada.

Re: Overdue Bill for Sundries, Final Notice.

Sir,

Having applied to you repeatedly but ineffectually for a settlement of my bill for clothes, liquor, and sundries, I have now to intimate that unless your account is paid in full before 12 o'clock tomorrow I shall place it in my solicitor's hands for recovery in a court of law.

I am, Sir,
Your obedient servant,

C. N. Skinner

Bishop Bompas in Chthonia

Fragment from the lost Daybook
of the Seer of the Kootenays.
Yukon Territory, 1 January, 1892.

1

Mundane egg cools on its plate.
Aether, Chaos, *soufléed* confusion,
strife (audience of wisdom) crackling, mirthless.
What view is this that picks me up like two hands
and sends me packing towards the metropolis but
    for the paintbrushes?
Where should I put this large bag of night with
    its black wings?
Where goes the second race of men to find their Jerusalem?
And how is it that they have clouds in their brains yet?

I have lost my faculty for increase and decrease,
and my material body loses its form; I have lost
the power for evil and the deceptions of idleness:
I am freed of illusions, of desire, of insatiable ambition,
arrogance and audacity, temerity, all out of me,
lost my wicked fondness for riches and pleasures,
and falsehood also gone out of me.

2

Thus purified, I stand in merit and force,
Pimander to counsel men to piety and wisdom.
Live soberly. Abstain from gluttony.
Fly the darkness of ignorance.
Withdraw from the light that obscures,
the heats that chill and jade,

escape from corruption.
Acquire immortality.
3
Well and good.
Easy to say.
The precepts of wisdom for all,
yet not for all.
The dross and the horn,
the mind of the universe
the day before *yestren,*
and all a brief pain,
or prolonged.
4
What do we say–O hands invisible
which buoy us up–to change night
into day, unknot the strange humour
of new forms and perishings that dull
hope with variousness and rue.

Mrs. Mary Coy Bradley

Coy Lake, New Brunswick, B.N.A.,
November 1817.

I have arrived at glory by slow degrees,
long entranced in the phantasmagoria of instants,
listening through the subtle and trivial roaring to the lion
of the Lord, who whispers messages of peace of mind.

The dark sinners and mild, distraught, or inclined
by nature or habit to excesses of movement,
to motion in no luminescence of regard for right,
nor to right understanding (that is, keen with love).

The blent cries front, behind, gnash the spent air
and roll out into nothing, unregarded by streamlets
gripped into convulsions of roiled snow,
by puppies, or by small children at ease with God.

I stand for this and that in baleful Friday,
unjust, self-incriminated, murdering Monday
with the selfishness common to days and nights,
slave of blood and hunger, life in death.

Many occasions I fail to escape temptation
on various accounts, causing darkness to envelope
my mind for a time. I stand in cold corners and bleat
remorse, a lamb of fear, crying out for a Master.

And then, in the cold winter: "Mary arise, the Master
is come, and calleth for thee." And weather

be what it may, I rise, rejoicing in the root cellar,
dancing amid the cloud of happy spirits with Christ.

I am the sister who calls out to you: "Pour out your heart
on your imperfections to God, but joyful shout *selah*!"
The God of all men holds wickedness in check with you,
the repentant are fat in the flourishings of the Lord.

The Hanging of Samuel Lount and Peter Matthews

Toronto, April 12, 1838.
for André Furlani.

While it must be allowed that mob is always
open to the introduction of the noose,
the general feeling within any assembly
remains with the victim, and tends in sympathy even
towards the judiciously hanged. Alike to other jostling ovals,

several hundreds assemble on Potters' Field,
a shallow rise north towards a stout, washed, block
of ten twelve-pane windows, eight more, like eyes,
staring off east, as if for blue Nova Scotia, or some
other kindly friend not so far from somewhere.

The knot of citizens thirty-six deep ripple
like Chelsea supporters, the moment settling
like an inevitable goal, the keeper's ears fluttering,
straining for a sound of reprieve so the dream of ending
should end, and the normal day rise quickly from gloaming.

But no day comes, and flickering scenes of wild talk
and mystic eloquences, the voice of fire and water,
and an end to banishment and disfavour, do not stay.
I wish the drop had been conceived, they might
have thought had they known, but a slow strangling

awaits not for Samuel. Poor Lount. Poor Matthews.
Frock coats of myriad hues of grey and brown,
hats, conical top-hats, creased as often as not,

a queer uprightness of the body in most,
though the standing crouch of age, and the use

of the stick for support, or effect, recollected
the fashion at Westminster or Whitechapel.
The rebel faction was not in conspicuous evidence,
though the Christian people murmured, and relatives
of the banished looked on shocked at the sudden turn.

The left rather than the right foot characterized the throes
of Lount: the queer kicking dance beyond all telling,
rhythmic, ultimately, a small vibration of a scuffed boot,
four barely distinguishable motions for retrial
registered at last resort, and with but attenuated success.

Too late, too late for poor Lount, for Matthews,
who might have loved, had he sense enough to choose aright–
and Alex, "What of Alex in his America?"

Montreal, 05.

Lawren Harris's "Garden"

A pale copy in gouache.

Geometry beset by blue powers, gales and biology,
black and white blent into brightening reds,
Albinoni at a gleeful remove echoing hollow
along my haunted hallway in Saint Martins,
b-flat minor fearfully skipped across the forever pond,
where the deer were a flicker of white on white,
so roseate lines might fix an inexpressible image, strong
even under my crude copying of Lawren Harris's garden,
its inexplicable rednesses against the cobalt straits,
disconnected flames behind stark birch, hale cedar,
the roof, preserved in oils, a series of subtle lines,
forcing the eye: recognition a sterile twitch,
all the more for that, *contact*; the note always b-flat minor,
the ineluctable, unswerving trueness we sometimes note
and press toward a moment to come, where we shall sound,
and be sound.

Remembering Aeneas McCharles

Boxer, reformed drunkard,
evangel.

By strange parachronism the primal leaps forward,
once again at the throat like the throttling beast He is,
when the past recurs to make melodious memory.
The oblique defense, the meta-chronicle,
is triangulation, and further geometrical discussion.
I follow the whorling spiral revealed in the detritus,
the dust in the air that is words, and words inscribed,
whisking away the grim bones into dancing again.

I hear a Montreal poet railing that Lawrence and Rimbaud
are the two only, who convey the duress of modern bestiality.
And the febrile chorus of the rest are to compose in Belsen
or some other place of horrors for thinking of somewhere else.
Through fragments of smoked meat, briefly the air of words
is again impelled smoothly across his tongue, forming
    his fragrant glottals,
labials, and dentals, into an unattenuated fog of mustard mist.

Laying a curtain in front of these odours, a stark memoir
of a long lost North Ontario purifies the air with sense.
In the library of volumes compelled by such isolation
the mind is revealed approaching nearer its uniformity,
and we detect the voice of the collective human
praying against rain and cold death, chastened.
Between conscience and a cold sheet, with bad teeth
to grow worse, the lightened load ever heavier,
until candid welcome greets one or another
in the long woods.

Whether cold cannibals
make cruelty out of song of wonder is a crooked stick
to lie with. Out of the bag come the round corners.
Windego, Weetigo, where have you gone, if not off
to attack a city with magic aircraft and wondrous weapons,
new ways of toasting flesh to black grit to sounds of weeping.
Gryphius wrote his Platonist hymns while Silesia writhed
in the gore of the world's perpetual wickedness,
revolving vowels and repeating consonants
while the foul and unholy sky opened over him.

But war even in solitude: a mother and daughter
who live on the mice who lived on thin father
in his posthumous ripening, his underside fresh beyond
the fire's short reach, while thrice the heavens turned
on their perpetual axis. Adrift in the still sea of winter
the air clean against corruption, an ice god consults
a Solar myth to find whether he will recover from his sickness.
But he is a thin father who hovers like the sharp snow
drifting over drift through the hard tints of Arctic aquamarine,
and will not be put so right again.

The Visitation of Margaret Blennerhasset, *Née* Agnew

Montreal 1819.

Fleeing history: into myriad-minded
alleys, *les oubliettes,* dusty cataracts
of whispering silences, crumbling
paper, the hope of a voice undoing

as the living mind elevates fragments
and by chance of training a singing out,
the hermeneutical subject unbound,
a Prometheus of lesser extent,

playing to sympathies and aesthetics
of syntax, a style revealing the whole
in a flicker, in her breast still life holding

a feeble sway, the widow of the Rock
haunting along thy green embowering woods,
in the colder Canada of the world.

The Haunting of Daniel O'Leary

The Pioneer Ulsterman's Table.

Cleansed of imperfections, the spirit of the mind
arranges herself across a well-planed face
of antique pine board: a pioneer table, sturdily crude,
perfect medium for spirit suspension,

a table-knocker's delight, in truth. Yet here the thrill
of airy contact persists, and without the overheated
enthusiast's wishing so hard as to be tossed over their hillock
of shrill and cold pretence. A ghost *enjoined,*

through motions of arms, arcs quickly attending
lumber chosen for sweep in the grain,
moments of perception in careful framing,
prominences of chance perfection.

Other qualities animated grow manifest,
touches added as the bias of form
emerged, trimmings augmenting transient
recognition, hypnogogic in geometries of pine.

Hard use of years has yet to efface the tenaciousness
of ten minute's thought while Victoria was girl-Queen,
and news from Belfast and Coleraine dire,
and our joiner gave thanks for this rather than that.
Attention a purity of selfhood confirmed by all,
overlapping spheres taking shape from shape, then,
now, documenting the self-written against time,
fragrant, luminous, distinct, and beyond naming.

Of Magi and Sage
James Evans, his *Quotidiana*,
Moose Factory, 1832

The way of knowing puts hand in hand of God, briefly.
The way keeps wolf from door, beast from house.

How to sustain one or another? Who stands ahead,
   ochre-faced,
in otter mantle reading from the Book of Answers?

Others forward as living ghosts, the Word,
the Dead, living on in the Good.

In stillness I cry out for those who are not,
clinging sometimes to relics and amulets.

In darkness I look out for thee, who seas
and mountains hold intangible as memory.

The Emigration of Whitechapel Bess

Off Nova Scotia, 1777.

The she-fiends of the Mollie dens and the flash houses,
the All-night Lads and the Peep-o-day boys at the
   Duke Of York,
the Cyprians in to Tom and Moll King's, or the King's Arms,
all tormented Covent Garden venereal, demented,
eight thousand copies of Harris's catalogue
retailing the allure of the scab and the slow-murdered wife,
the startled boy and his yellow discharge, chancres
boding ill, the hundreds of thousands of buttocks and twang,

each their world away from five-pound passage to anywhere:
I watch the redcoats in and out, pray, bathe
in too little water: alert to desperate need Jack
and brother John cling to purses and to pence,
decayed cullies groping with breech-buttons one-handed,
the other guarding fob with black nails ungently urgent,
and the wheedling of a fading child but the keen,
the savour, in the late scenes of rank career.

Capax deitatis, the rare surprise of providence a boon,
I am lifted up to the Lord by an open hand,
I sing hymns and drift into drab clothes and holy speech,
exhorting. The mobbed rabble push past to put the boot in,
and I am not afraid. Your bluecoats in tight formation square
and draw their beads, each soul effigy graven in torn flesh
and wasted sanctuary. The home is a sanctuary, and here
is a marbled temple, if a home is to bless and enjoy blessing.

I preach the way of ways on the boards of a rolling deck,
the Gloucester Quaker skipper assembling hands:

I have no ship and I have a ship, I am a glass for seeing,
there is no temple and the temple is built, here, where,
knowing suffering, you will have power not to suffer.
I sleep on cold plank and arise renewed, elemental
desires fed on air, on the fire of the Lord of all means.
The pains I have felt in my fear intensify, yet I am whole.

The malignancies and powers rising rough from greys
over the gunwhales, wailing as if a gale blew,
and the ship of wood were but a ship of wood,
and the devils and spectres of spindrift howled nothing
of the rotted beds of the wrecks of Whitechapel and St Giles,
of maidens who heard dark bargains struck for liberties,
freedom for decrepit lusts and poxing caresses, forcing,
cajoling briefly, in shows of sentiment brief and sharp.

A line, a sheet, stays sails of discourse inspired by saints,
on these and other themes of stiffened resolve and
    suffering right,
and I hear my voice cry out that the word of God in
    each generosity
claims a creed of charity, that the beast in the press is undone,
and the myriad-faced power of crime and despair is lain down,
and we kneel in our need on the gentle deck on water calmed,
singing to the lap organ, making signs of our thanksgiving
that the voyage has returned us safe, into a safe land,
    homeland.

Whig Histories

Millennial Poem for Canada

Point Grey, British Columbia, August, 2000.

As I stride along, my muscles taut and young,
shoulders square, without pain or fear,
a tree rises in me and I feel a blazing out,
a cone of light rising perfected into a golden pine.
The athletic tree gambols up the shady lane–
antlers waving through the bush my branches come,
an answer to death delivering its wild night of blank divinity.

Begun a faun, the maddened satyr ages yet to wisdom,
while all below is whispering: what say you now, love.
The crazy forest where all is well is delivered in bland
infinitude. What news the Great Lone Land I know not,
I am in this blizzard of presence, and my mind cannot
    be there.

I begin to resemble what I am not–cedar,
William Blake,
a brown trout, a mossy curve in a lost trail, skin, bones.
And I am kinder than I was, to cedars deferential.
I am lifted geometric on haunches of strong muscle,
rooting through Baffin drift to mind the stern horizon,
the cold bloom, my angel, against the deep winter dark.

Strange Songs

"I am glad to be on *terra firma* again.
"It is only a *de facto* government.
"Black on white and *vice versa.*
"He returned to this *alma mater.*
"He talked *ad libitum, ad nauseam,* and *ad infinitum.*"

In the aftermath of my learning
from the Saducees that there was to be
no resurrection, I telephoned and reserved
a place on an excursion to the Northern Occident,
up Newfoundland's western coast,
beyond the White, and then Hare Bay,
then north past Port Burwell
towards the Hudson Strait.

It is now plain that distress was my compass,
but I would find a Hyperborean sage,
a magician dragged out of a callow sketch
stolen from Hesse or Daumal,
a bay man Bodhisattva.

Self-righteousness that knows no bounds,
foolishness and carnality that knows only extremity:
it is not easy to forgive our own stupidities.
So I lay on a deckchair remembering.
Eo instanti, my tongue arches in the saying
of "Good *Maistre,* how shall I know *La Vie Éternelle?*"

Subtle as a parrot, abstruse as a Cardinal,
knowing nothing of the work of years,
we have before us a criminal who confesses.
But even now, in this changed state, I recall
him standing, the origin of speech and thought,
like a new cadence, or a fresh facet on a gem.

With my book of questions, I took a lighter
up the fjord leading north to Baffin's upper reaches,
to an igloo of grey stones, a world of lichen.
Between the talent and the talisman,
a kind of no and a sort of yes, a hill
that won't be climbed, a river of foolish water.

In Inuit, Cree, Irish, Norse, Basque and French,
he looked for English that might be shaped
to sense, impromptu, as he passed us smoked *floki,*
and savoured motes of bone salt, considering,
no doubt, some fine point of Hyperborean
ornamentation, four arms of a cross broken upward.

Quell the mould, heart-mould, wander of mind
across mouldy afterthought, odour
of the mould, of mouldering, evacuate mould,
casting the mind forward to the mind of mould,
which is no mind, but the last secretion of body,
clinging, a vibration of lesser flesh.

Anti-poem One: Introductory

Willie Yeats and Charlie Roberts in Happy Valley, Labrador.

Poetry—a void around a void.
The world is too various.
In what respect is the mind moved forward
in jotting this or that abstraction.
From the street I hear as a shred of conversation:
"Time and space do not refer to entities."
What am I to make of that?
Verse is never free: I am thinking
in particular of the ghost of Charles G. D. Roberts
scribbling notes on the margins of Canada's
first and forgotten modernist poet, disinterred
long enough to recollect the scribbling
of wry notes *by a hand older in this game.*

The ceiling is not amply extended, though the same gas
accumulates. The barking of dogs maintains a ragged pitch.
Several other fictional contemplations of the poet occur
in rapid procession.

And to what end the glass of god in shards,
Ontario from the sky.
For a race of snow angels,
sawing the wood when there is wood to be sawed,
but drawing no attention to themselves.
Manitoba, I have crawled on my belly through your bogs
in an August of mosquitoes:
winters we kept warm.

I will and channel poems and a Laurentian spout
cascades a very verse of a deathless Labrador Yeats,
a Yeats shorn of interferences, of blather and posturing,
pristine in obscurity. I lift this poet
from the brown rock with careful tweezers.
Rhodomanthys, fingers of flame,
gutter on the Baffin horizon, deep cobalt
giving up its stars to the inhuman cold.

I will worship the cold, not poetry.
Cold to keep a howling at bay–
a howling over the land like that of wolves,
and subtle in its measure.
Do not take on the burden
of hearing these beasts or they will turn,
and we become Khazars of the North,
re-fashioned after the image of the *US*
we must become to suit them,
to suit us for them.

Ice of the fierce drift of seas,
the true headstone fissured with the only name,
a signature signed with weather,
praying our Soul into being.

Anti-poem Two:
The Visions of Harold Adams Innis

The disposition of the times invited
meditation on the economic significance of material culture.
What is this writhing thing if not the ongoing collapse
of Western Civilization, which started in 1900,
or so H.A.I. said in 1934.

But what of transportation?
A ship's documents from Georgian Bermuda.
Butter manifests—a very mouthful of the past.
How this desperate seeking into the void
and its desert of paper for a clue to a present
dilemma?

Void, vacuum, nullity, emptiness: variations
on an endless if vacuous theme. But, as our hero
informed the Canadian Political Science Association
in May of 1931, the Ottawa and St. Lawrence routes
had to be unified before the canoe and the lake boat
could move in concert, and only after 1760

can the strange force be said to have begun
which moves over the *nation* like snow clouds,
or clouds of methane over a planet of gas.
So we have two forces:
a collapse of the West,
and the rise of Canada; to play its bit part
in the rivalry of peoples for economic advantage.

Anti-poem Three:
On the Logic of Deep Time

Act. The dead herring and the perpetual charm of geometry. The upper Fraser is home to a small child. The ancient blue of Quebec City, a nude or a plant left inadvertently in the forest. The red rose is the most abstract of horse tracks in the snow. The widow's hands are also folded, white planes rift the backwoods into the hills above Margaree. Like totem poles, three sisters guard the church at low tide. The large wooden puffin waits. Aroused to frenzy by the sudden disfigurement I arise towards my crisis. There are bands of colour and a knot of pilgrims under an Otter banking over a square. HMCS Athabaskan rolls, is gone.

The forest fire gives way to the Saskatchewan river: I am alone briefly. When the shelter is complete, this is not so. An old repeater, once used for moose in Labrador, is traded to a Wood Cree for a road through a pair of hills in the Miramachi. I wait here. The trees, unmoved, burst into factories that are no longer prose like the wounded elk at his goring. The dog sled moves on. It is difficult yet to recall the vain sky that John knew then. The basket is no mountain when the mask slips. A row of fences. In five years, the soil and gravels of the bank will give way, revealing the planking and lank costume of long ago. Her glacier is a house at thrust faults–the bog that runs downhill. I track across this snow to Povungnituck, where I find snow and a bag filled with inner and outer garments. But what meaning in this view of two clay pots? *Vvvv*

Anti-poem Four:
Eyelash under the Eyelid

The freedom to speak one's mind is the first concession of the student prostrating will and effort at the altar of professional achievement. Since one's history of error has become an habitual preoccupation of the psyche in her search first for success or fame, and then–in wiser years–for warm feet, all improvement tends toward the self-censoring, self-chastisement of the grammarian and empiricist. I would be better that I change my life for the better is an apothegm liable of upset in the chaos of winds. The tootler on whistles, the poet, and the fanciful architect give way to the reformed mind, which nonetheless continues to wrestle in a confusion. What to do, what to do?

Scholarship is a treacherous balm, half a salve of wisdom, half an unctuous lure into lucrative professions that hobble the mind with clerkship and round meals. And wiser more for an appreciation of grease on the gums. But how cool feels the Autumn when Lucretia sings her orison, observes the intuitive man. In age we learn more from children, realize that we grow stupid in preparation for redemption, or not, of earlier promise. And between here and there is a forest of pains. Most die in its wood, perplexed and winded, or drunk.

The brutal thought is a great mercy also to the benighted mind, violence smoothing a thousand subtle scrupulosities, inviting a hundred pleasures, each with its own maze of phases of laughter. What to do, what to do? Repeat thyself as long as is decent, then pray to Heaven for largesse in lieu of largeness. The repetition of work, the Tuesday after Monday, the window behind the laptop: all conspire to reduce doubt to stasis, abasement and its postures in the sudden rain. I am maimed by the child standing before this suffering future, as if I must go through my pain again, and so it is.

But the beauty of life buoys the sleepiest relic. An hour in a copse of sugar maples, a minute of play with a son or daughter, surprised on the street by an old friend, we rise into life like animals, welcoming the sap as it rises, as if it were more than it is, and they and we were to be spared.

Catholicon: a Universal Remedy

Against Maltreatment of Children.

For the Millenium,
the Rising of the Moon,
and the Marching Season.
And for R. Christ.

When handling the book,
pause to ablute the hands.
Approaching the book,
cradle the spine in clean palms.

Open the boards suavely,
a gentle gesture of ninety degrees:
open-faced, but not splayed.
Now, look frankly to the type.

In all gentleness, do you hear
the voice that calls for mayhem?
Much to forgive, and bad as the other,
does that voice also say, *one more time*?

In which book are such things written?
Not, "the blood which has been a torrent,"
but, *more* blood, more children, for the maw
of a grim, singing, beast.

In my book I nurse a grave-hedge
of cedar and mercy, and forgiving,
I am forgiven. I forget that this book
was written by that bigot, Kingsley;

Or that it might have been some other's,
who suffered also throes of weakness,
yet said, *"Nothing is so dear,*
as pennilessness, nothing so anxious,

as carelessness, and every duty, bidden
to wait, returns with seven others, sharp
at its back." In my book, I haunt my lips
with, "to be happy we must be kind."

But in that other book it must say
other things, about malice, succulent,
like a roasted dog. It must opine,
that Miss Nangfou should face indoors.

A Man Talks to Himself Versified

The Poet's Arrival.

I'm not just saying this because I love you,
but you are truly great. Magnificent
in every respect, except one–your vanity
being immodestly small. Resplendent
the room in which you appear, shining
in yet another well-told anecdote
of scrape, exploit, or spree, taller
than your merely earthly span: noble.

When you have moved your mind away from
passion, and come back to yourself,
there is a shining I am ennobled to see.
I risk pocketing specimens from your comb
of your exceeding fine hair; odours
have also a certain something each to each.
A measure of the kidney: biliousness,
lubriciousness, an extra pint of porter.

Cobalt: An Alternative to Space Programs

More and more I am Vladimir.
–Walid Bitar

It is to be regretted
that the delusion foisted
on the public by the lunar-landing
hoaxes are so generally suffered
that we may never know
the true inhabitants of the Moon.

In their odd green hats
they cavort on the lush foothills
around Pico, singing their staves
in an unintelligible jargon
not so very far distant
from the Hungarian.

And though not gentle creatures,
and much given over to vices
identical to our own,
they may be seen also, after
their roasted lamb and stewed crane,
reading at Stoical repose.
Their philosophical volumes
tell of the aridity, of the deadening
gravity of the Earth, of its cheerless
solitude in which no beetle beetles,
and no microbe bends in the murk
or muck of liquid water:

a dizzying surface speed produced
by the Earth's diurnal motion
is said to account for its vast
cobalt plains, poisonous mists
twisted into tornadoes to slap massy
volcanoes at the flame of margins.

Imagine the wonder of the Lunar tribes
were we to construct a Siberian triangle,
whose sides of sequenced strobes would join
points five hundred versts distance from one another,
a prodigy risen from our desert world
unmistakable in its triple greeting.

The Concubinage and Fornication
of Phantom and Grub

A careful, considering man is half a conjurer.
And where honesty rules, the mind chastises the body.

Composed, I am become a cube.
The Tree of the World
lowers branches laden.
Raphael lit by wings of flame
points to the treat of flesh.

I would say more in what I have not said.
This word, that word, each a sphere
devoid of response, a death nothing.

Of one succession of days I say
that beyond the Himalayas
is far away indeed, and Thule
requires a boat I an unable to build
easily.

I lift my arms to repair the damage.
Standing erect, fingers up, palms together,
elbows at the level of my ears.

In my mind, multitudinous maps, life-size
and contiguous, swarm with the *eidolona*
of minds that make maps, and resound
with the motets and jingles appropriate
to cartographies and glyphs of sylph-hood.

Thou worm, saith the careful man,
knoweth the earth no better today
than yesterday, so consider thy state.

Crowning of the Virgin

There is an enormous force that runs through me.
Sometimes it is an ancient face at the end of a tunnel,
eyes like a gnome, or a faery out of Chretien de Troyes:
abloat and glistening, topped in a skin cap,
staring at some new wonder wrought in iron.

I feel pain in my side, but as I consider
that wise man and fool find terminus in the earth,
I find my heart soar, the beauty of the world becoming
another of the masks of what no tongue speaks.

But I cannot live with this: it is stressful
to meet many Buddhas, and the Buddha of pleasure
has many tongues; the world Buddha here,
where complaisant Buddhas trade slogans, posturing
enlightenment, posing as curious, before adultery.

One Buddha said that Christ had gone, and as two angels
took form of immaculate men, chaste or chastened,
watching for such as I was then: *O the broom,
the bonny, bonny broom.* Two palms touch as miracle.
Peace gives another new body to breathe in.

In the Early Times of Which We Speak

On a plain in the land of Shinar.

The grave is bottomless.
Our cycles of pleasure,
deceit, failure, and abjection,
are as little as our love for ourselves,
and the urn has no inside;

afflatus, hope, and affection,
excitement, study, and intemperance,
as little as immediate cessation of all stimuli,
followed by an absence of all qualities.

The long way around is that god
dies and dies and dies.
And the elegant minutiae
of the myriad-minded world,
and its inelegant slump
when the mind closes,
is but an immense series
of meaningless complications,
driven by some force
immense, random, and unthinking.

When seawater splashes into a boot,
and November seems a cold enough month,
or a lifted arm becomes sticky with spilt coffee,
and the phone is heavy with tidings,
when a glass of water's your man,
and bent cards tremble in hands palsied,
another river rising from stillness
will glassily conclude: completed,

convoluted ramifications of perspective
enact polygons of force, enwrap
the brain a green cricket, vary
degrees of cold in moons and men.

Singing desperately a beautiful music
a broken finch warns finches of a cat.
Her poems are not for today, her lyric
is in the dust over amygdaloidal porphyry,
a thousand millenia of atoms fled
from this monad who in last thought
was a finch warning finches.

Maybe I will rise and face the decades,
and swim to find submarine hills littered
with the collapse of columns of marble,
and a ruin of a temple of laughter
where death is much beaten by waves.

Here the fretted ripple markings
along silt are glyptic, tidal movement
absently drawing sand into figures,
characters that remember everything,
and intone at the touch the everlasting.

Guessing the Devil's Age

A diverse class, the assembled pupils;
each strongest at the wild spit of ignorance,
looking for America north of its border,
and *charmant* withal, but for peculiarities
attendant upon having ended up here.

Our pedagogy occurs as in a fable–
the wizard, a frog among storks, lives out
so many deaths as pass by his eyes to enchant
with this and that retelling of two eyes open.

The world pours as time through an ear of shell.
I can hear the ocean, like an empty room.
Other like commonplaces, until hoarse,
batrachian, silence fills the wearied room.

Discard your gills and tail–there is freedom.
A tale to storks if to storks e'er tale there was.
Tom Tit Tot from the Carnatic to Mush-a-mush,
rude holes in stone to let the dead out.

With every other mark of brutality and hope,
proud, covetous, wanton, envious, idle thoughts
come from myself, or out of the road of my corruption.
Here, I guess the greatness of other kings by my own.

Dressed in Blue and Green

Every highway is a dead zone.
The hanged men dangle unnamed, un-owned–
below decks, or spiking a railway,
inconvenienced by a yardarm,
adrift in Cadiz.

At fourteen a galley hand off Baffin,
and at Beechey staring at the starkness.
Those were times. Char and *d'aventure*.
Death all about and the stony air swollen
near with voices, a residue wild laughter
and mad hope.

Grief and grievances crowd
the back of a horde of sins:
the quick shivies, and the careful timer,
the boot in the gut of that fat Yank chief
who drank to Tirpitz in Sierre Leone.

On highways the craft goes on,
pistols and petrol; refined feeling
a package of rare cigarettes, or a stiletto
spat from a statue of the Virgin
on a British Carrier at Cagliari, Sardinia.

There was a place. No roads for wheeled carts
until 1828, and feudal thirty years more.
Giant's graves, malaria, and higher ground,
and Gerrie and Mick and Jocko, no mess at present,
scabrous bones, barely tended by the priests.

O bring me back home to nowhere,
'twas nowhere that I'd right to be;
and nowhere to nowhere I'll wander,
and between ply a trade on the sea.

I'll wrap all my treasures in linen,
coarse stuff I can have by the yard,
I'll drop with a stone to the bottom,
trussed up, and to nowhere so hard.

The Chief P.O. sleeps in his last fart,
his hover of foul dust like must in an old book.
His sons have new fathers now, his daughters
endangered or married, while he's a box of worms,
an Ark Royal promotion, Chief Lungs-Gone Stoker.

The difference between the dark and the rain
is a coracle upturned, and raw fingers
a paralysis of hurt in holes torn through tar.
Drowning becomes no great matter when
the sleep is so very very deep. Wakey, Wakey.

On a Theme by P. H. Gosse

Beyond Evenings at the Microscope.

Not to intrude on a privacy so recluse,
but the slough of the eyes
presents one of the most exquisite objects
that you can behold.

Pear-shaped *exuviæ,* the facetted
portions are well defined in blue,
each facet varying accordingly
as the perfectly hexagonal outline,
the glossy convexity, comes into focus.

This vessel, now and then,
at irregular intervals,
dilates quickly and closes;
the wave proceeding upward
toward the head, but only
for a short distance,
unattended with an impulse
of the blood globules.
Stirred, I leave the body.

Not All Poets Are Fools

The study of the archives proves only
human wickedness.
Of our senses, five are obscured.
An event of occultation, distortion
borne of the born human:
the scent of the fig blossoms,
of paradise occluded
by the stench of our disorder.

How should I prove such a thing?
Should I prove such a thing?
I feel a small hillock of brain
sprout out over the bracken of brow,
snug in helmet of new cranial horn.
I am swifter of speech now so.

What a prospect my evolution brings
as the cataracts of human being
scale, find light blue, and the rest.
Old Self would have paused here, tarried
out of idleness or perpetual self-indulgence–
but the being that looks back on Old Self

breaks off the tongue that says no to toil.
It is laborious sprouting lobes of brain
says (facts as no human sagacity could have
forseen) *sensus communis,* no soil for days,
not such as this plant flourishes in, no palate
for the buoyancy of these novel flavours.

Of Whig Histories

A Dissertation to Prove the Uncertainty of Physic,
and the Danger of Trusting Our Lives to Those Who
 Practise It.

Write your own history daily:
there is no darkness so deep as that of the mind.
Enquire within upon everything.

To soften the skin
and improve the complexion,
flowers of sulphur
mixed in a little milk
let stand an hour, and
without disturbing a bloom,
the milk rubbed into the skin.

Eyelashes may be lengthened
by clipping their tips
once a month, a practice
never failing in desired effect.

An effervescence ensues,
once more I am reminded that persons
who suffer from rheumatism,
or have a tendency to it,
should not drink cider.
But be to every servant a friend,
and heartless, indeed,
will be the servant who does not warm
in love to you.

Avoid manifestations of ill-temper,
avoid pride, and affectation is a form of pride,
avoid telling idle tales.

To make Senna and Manna palatable,
stew a quarter ounce of each
in a pint of boiling water,
and pour the infusion
over a half a pound of prunes,
and two large dollops
of West India molasses.

With two hundred years of soil
on my tongue, chips of skullcap,
and fragments of filthy hair,
I am into the wind.

Karkara

The question of style is the question of meaning. What can it mean to say, "I have collected all together. All together. And have considered all. I have considered all, and find that all was only the half of it."

Nothing. It can mean nothing.

If I say "Furnivall," at least you know what I mean.

"Great is the Lord, and marvellous, worthy to be praised; there is no end of his greatness," and you get a clear picture.

"I ease nature, and discharge my belly," you attend an observation patently redundant, but doubly clear in amber.

To have collected all together, and said so, is to have given witness to one's own moderated dilation of perspective, and to have precipitated a ragged and derisory chorale of, "all what?"

The risible mob is best left to its traditional devices of wrack and ruin.

Best to have not spoken of all, at all, at all.

And such a story would not be written in a straight line.

Under each letter, would be a series of momentary considerations: faces, facets, facetiæ, facilities, facilitations, fæces.

Favours like a line of Old Norse *runhende,* running right into its rhyme with diphthongs that leave them long blinking.

I gasp at the smell. All sweat and whale grease.

The metaphysics of the more of the same. And when you want it,

instead of always a hundred miles from the party and stinking of bad fish.

Dulse, dulse, and dulse for afters, spiced with dulse.
Karkara.
My prison is made by the voice of the tern.
Karkara, karkara.

X=Y

Oppression makes itself inevitable.
The sea oppresses the land and the glories
of the white city on the heights
tumble splintered along centuries of tidal shelf,
silts enrobing the lobster gut, easing
transitions, erasures, and tidal serendipities.

I take responsibility:

for systems and structures relating to all aspects
of society referred to and referenced by established Law
and Legal Custom, warranted by the Head of State,
and protected by the Security Forces, Bureaucracy,
and Governmental Apparatus as Constitutionally sanctioned;

for all future use of security systems or networks
organized to protect
subjects from terrorizing cartels and dangers
associated with ungoverned acquisition;

for the cracked cobble and the whole;

for the angle of perihelion, and redness in apples,
for uniformity of rhubarb leaves.

I am worn with the load of it all.

Frederick Edward Smyth's 1911 Centenary Lecture

On Zen, Sir Peter Topsail, Trade Unions,
and the Fundamental Rightness
of Bicameral Parliamentarianism.

My Lords. Ladies. Gentlemen. And others.
[A modest tittering amid the thin audience].

If I may begin, begin with quotation,
with quotation of Sir Peter–

(not calculated to inspire friendly feeling
in all toward his Lordship I'm afraid).

Sir Peter said in a speech before parliament:
"Back benchers. Back benchers must,
must represent much,
much to their own distaste, disgust even,
while aiming at private secretary,
finally to be a king…
but then, not really a king.

Only those who lived before the French Revolution
can truly be said to have seen the sunlight or witnessed
moonshine.

Then England was England."

Even now, as I said last evening
(much to my Whip's consternation),

the Cabinet, the Cabinet has little influence,
little influence on the coteries, the coteries
surrounding, surrounding Prime Ministers,

as four perhaps friendly cats circle
a dazed mouse.

Nor can we neglect to point out Sir Peter's
many, many, warm friendships.
His hospitality towards working-class women,
whom the Times reports as having kept portraits,
portraits of Sir Peter under their pillows.

And perhaps especially in some defense
of Sir Peter's contention
that the sum total of human happiness,
knowledge, and achievement,
would have been unaffected, had

the songs of Sappho,
Joan of Arc's dreams,
Mr. Browning's poems,
the novels of George Eliot,
and all their like,
been boiled in a cocked hat.

Sir Peter adds, "The world would be different
not one iota."

It will assuage few suffragettes
to know that Sir Peter was prompt
in gracious allowance of generation,
its acts, and the performance of women
as perpetuators of the species.

[shuffling of papers,
grimaces of confusion, the clerk's text swimming]

.... Sir Peter's mother was once heard to remark,
"Two and two might not be four
under the authority of the right stick."

And Churchill... no,
Sir Peter, yes, Sir Peter...
Sir Peter had rapidly risen to an Earldom,
yet was no fawning pup of Lords

(but he was pleased, *aye, pleased,*
when with Churchill and Lloyd George
and Asquith... no,
just Asquith, and Lloyd George...),

yes. that's it.

[mopping his brow,
papers in a sudden scattering borne
of the palsy of failing nerve]

I mean to say, to say that's when Sir Peter's coalition,
Sir Peter's coalition, managed,
managed to break the trade unions

(who in fairness, it must be said,
frequently caused unnecessary problems),

managed to kick Paddy between his teeth,
and whack votes for women
into the wine-dark seas.

But in 1919 Sir Peter's heart had changed,

and he bellowed loud *Huzzahs!* at the news
that women had been given the *boat*.
They had earned it by then, you see.

(He was quite right. There can be no doubt about that.)

[*With a wistful glance at a small scatter of youthful female faces,
nervously, hopefully, gamely grinning out of set jaws,
chuckling briefly, and a little early.*]

And we'll see about those Irish,
see if we don't.

Afterwards, Sir Peter always was nostalgic
for England before 1914.
Tallyrand it was who said
one hadn't lived if one had not been in France
before the Revolution.

And England
was never the same after 1814.
1914, I meant to say, rather.
Or rather 1814. Yes, 1814.

But then again. Nothing ever changes.
The same problems. The same reform
of the House of Lords.
Thank Heaven for that at least.

Westminster (1 Feb).

A Laugh at Ludwig Wittgenstein: Dead Relations at Oxford

I saw you across the common at the Midsummer feast.
You held hands with two others in the ring.
You wore the blue jumper and looked distracted,
as if *trying* to be *there,* and so you were for a moment.

The world divides into facts: the strength of a belief
is not like the intensity of a pain, and a belief is not
like a momentary state of mind, the sun and stars are believed
into permanent and transient existences, and you stir,

out of your urn and rise up, taking the hands of strangers,
dancing at the feast for all and none but me to see.

Oxford, July, 1999.

Notes to the Poems

"Of the Decadent Poets"
Under the name Ajax, Wilfred Lalonde (born in Sainte-Marthe de Vaudreuil in 1876) contributed to the *Nationaliste,* the *Journal de Françoise,* and *Passe-Temps* in the early years of the twentieth century. His modesty ensured his current obscurity.

"The Mirror of Days (1897–1924)"
After 1897, when he was nineteen, Albert Lozeau lived his life as a paraplegic, long confined and seldom able to escape his room. He did, however, observe the Montreal of his day from his balcony, and enjoyed the blessing of friendship with his only intimate, the poet Charles Gill.

"After Anne Hébert"
This important poet was born in Sainte-Catherine-de-Fossambault in 1916, later fleeing in 1950 to Paris in order to escape an as yet intolerant and authoritarian Quebec. She returned to live in Montreal in 1997, dying there in 2000.

"Documents from the Office of Professor Darey"
I intend the "documents" here presented as a hermeneutic exercise, or case study, to show the strange manner in which individual documentary specimens of unrelated genres or types of language contexts relate hidden personal and psychological facts when juxtaposed. In this case, the extract from P. J. Darey's *Dominion Phrase Book* is substantially as it stands in the 1871 Dawson Brothers Montreal edition. Darey was a friend of the Dawson family, a family famous as geologists, surveyors, linguists, and academics.

"Bishop Bompas in Chthonia"
Born in 1834, Bishop William Carpenter Bompas was consecrated first Church of England Bishop of Athabasca in May, 1874.

In 1884, Bompas also became first Bishop of Mackenzie River, and in 1891, inaugural Bishop of Yukon. Bompas lived an extremely frugal and trying life for an established church bishop. He traveled thousands of miles by canoe and on horseback, living off the land, and enjoying the warm affection of Canadian Christians both of settler and native culture. Of Bompas, Bishop Whipple is said to have exclaimed ecstatically, "I know your great Bishop Bompas, and I tell you that the Apostles are living yet." Bompas died in 1906. Pimander, properly Poimandres, is an eponymous heresiarch and arch-wizard, source of a chapter, or fiction of a mystagogue, from the *Corpus Hermeticum.* Pimander may simply be another mask of the author known more commonly as Hermes Trismegistus.

"Mrs. Mary Coy Bradley"

Born in Grimross, New Brunswick, in September, 1771, Mrs. Mary Coy Bradley was one of Canada's greatest Christian feminists, an evangelical mystic whose fervour recollected Isaac Watt and William Blake. Her first husband David Morris died in March of 1817. Two years later she would marry Leverit Bradley, and under the name Mrs. Mary Coy Bradley preached and served as an inspired social activist among the Atlantic British Americans. The poem describes an autumnal crisis when, freed from her grief, Mary finds boldness in repentance.

"The Hanging of Samuel Lount and Peter Matthews"

Farmers and co-conspirators of Alexander Mackenzie, Samuel Lount and Peter Matthews, were hanged for treason in Toronto on April 12, 1838.

"Remembering Aeneas McCharles"

Boxer, Ontario pioneer, mining engineer, public benefactor, and raconteur, Aeneas McCharles was born in Cape Breton,

Nova Scotia, of Highland Scotch heritage. His autobiography is another of the neglected classics of early Canadian literature. In the poem, McCharles' spirit or *pneuma*–or better his ψυχή (psyche)–conditions a response in the present, uncontained by what Heidegger called "temporal being" or *being-in-time*.

"The Visitation of Margaret Blennerhasset"

Margaret Agnew Blennerhasset was born in Britain in 1771, a daughter of Robert Agnew, lieutenant governor of the Isle of Mann. She left Britain for North America under the shadow of having married her uncle Harman Blennerhassett. In 1819, Harman joined the Lower Canadian bar, having come to Canada after fleeing the United States when nearly bankrupt. After returning to Guernsey, Margaret was widowed in 1831, but died in New York in 1842 while pressing a case for financial compensation for earlier financial losses. Her "Widow of the Rock" is her best-known poetic work, but it is primarily of psychological and historic interest.

"Of Magi and Sage, James Evans, his Quotidiana, Moose Factory, 1832"

Born in Yorkshire in 1801, linguist, evangelist, and northern traveller James Evans immigrated to Lower Canada with his parents in 1822. Converted by the charismatic Methodist evangelist William Case, Evans and his wife joined the early settlers of Rice Lake, Upper Canada, as a teacher in a school for Indian children before moving on to Red River and eventually farther north to Norway House and Rossville, the Indian village where he developed his syllabic script for Ojibwa and Cree. His efforts at promoting his new system of writing led to nearly universal literacy among these tribes. In 1844, while in the Athabasca country to counter Roman Catholic activities, Evans accidentally shot and killed interpreter and teacher Thomas Hassall. From that point Evans became mercurial and visionary. Like William Blake, Evans' innocence was full blooded, and his fostering of young native women led to charges, flatly denied, of sexual misconduct. Although found innocent when he faced the charges in London, he died in England in 1846.

"The Emigration of Whitechapel Bess"
Born in Kilkhampton, Cornwall, in 1761, Elizabeth Grenfell moved to London in 1774. Forced into prostitution soon after, first in Westminster and later in Whitechapel, Bess was converted near Covent Garden in 1776 by a follower of John Wesley, immigrating to Nova Scotia in 1777. On the voyage, she experienced *gnosis,* and born again, arrived in Halifax at the moment of the great Loyalist exodus there. Taken up in the fervour of the Nova Scotian Great Awakening, Bess preached the gospel and mixed with likes of Henry Alline and Mary Coy Bradley.

"Anti-poem Two: The Visions of Harold Adams Innis"
Canadian nationalist and professor Harold Adams Innis (1894–1952) was one of the great historians of the twentieth century and needs little introduction here. Innis's method of arguing inductively, rather than ideologically, on the basis of extensive analysis of neglected archival documents, ultimately led to a critique of especially the American empire through a deep understanding of imperial communications. Influencing his famous younger colleague Marshall McLuhan's thought, and anticipating Jacques Ellul's radical studies of propaganda and technology, Innis's works continue to inspire Canadian technological nationalist resistance.

Daniel O'Leary's poetry has appeared in *Exile*, *Fiddlehead*, the spoken-word anthology *Poetry Nation*, and in numerous other journals. O'Leary is also a professor of Canadian Studies in the Department of English at Concordia University in Montreal. Aside from an earlier book of poetry, *The Sorcerer of Les Trois Freres*, he has published work on early Canadian print culture in The History of the Book in Canada and is co-editor with Jonathan Wisenthal of *What Shaw Really Wrote About the War*, a collection of previously unpublished prose essays by George Bernard Shaw. O'Leary is also editor of *Message to Eire: An Historical Anthology of Irish-Canadian Literature*, published by DC Books in 2010. A descendant of early Maritime Canadian families, O'Leary was born on the Fundy coast of New Brunswick, and was raised there and in Nova Scotia.